THE OFFICIAL
LIVERPOOL FC
ANNUAL 2002

YOU'LL NEVER WALK ALONE

LIVERPOOL
FOOTBALL CLUB

EST·1892 ®

"Never mind
the contract,
just give
me the team"
BILL SHANKLY

CARLTON
BOOKS

This is a Carlton Book

Published in association with Granada Media Commercial
Ventures

First published in 2001 by Carlton Publishing Group

10 9 8 7 6 5 4 3 2 1

A CIP catalogue record for this book is available from the British
Library

ISBN 1 84222 456 5

Text by Mark Williams; additional material by Wayne Cyrus and
Nick Moore and graphic design by Martin Port for Haymarket

Photographic Credits: Allsport, Action Images, Empics,
PA Photos, Steve Orino, Mark Leech, Anton Want

Printed and bound in Italy

Carlton Publishing Group
20 Mortimer Street
London W1T 3JW

THE OFFICIAL
LIVERPOOL FC
ANNUAL 2002

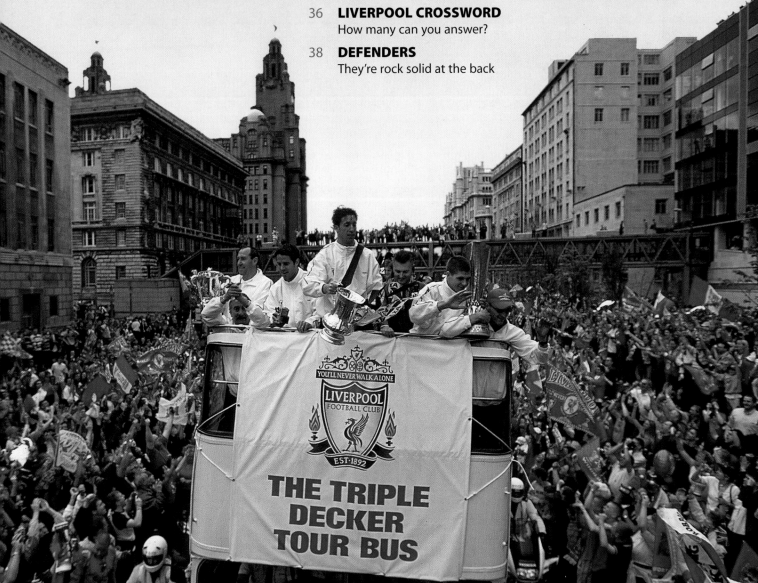

THE TRIPLE
DECKER
TOUR BUS

WELCOME...

TO THE OFFICIAL LIVERPOOL FC ANNUAL 2002

With the Reds winning a unique cup treble and also qualifying for the Champions League, what a truly amazing season 2000/01 was for Gérard Houllier's men.

You'll find all the reports and action-packed pictures from last season's historic campaign right here in this annual. Your favourite players are profiled, together with the manager and coaches. We'll show you behind the scenes of Anfield on matchday and we'll take a look inside the Liverpool Academy. You'll also get tips on how to improve your game and we'll test how much you really know about the Reds.

In short – everything a young Liverpool fan needs to know.

Let's start by looking ahead to next season. Fill in the table below every week to keep a record of the Reds' Premiership results.

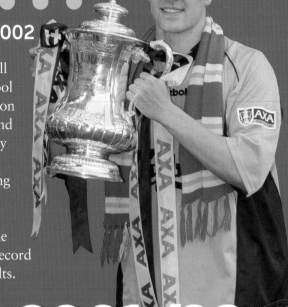

PREMIERSHIP 2001/02

DATE	OPPOSITION	RESULT	SCORERS	★ STAR MAN
18.8.2001	v West Ham United			
27.8.2001	Bolton Wanderers			
8.9.2001	v Aston Villa			
15.9.2001	v Everton			
19.9.2001	v Fulham			
22.9.2001	v Tottenham Hotspur			
29.9.2001	v Newcastle United			
13.10.2001	v Leeds United			
20.10.2001	v Leicester City			
24.10.2001	v Southampton			
27.10.2001	v Charlton Athletic			
3.11.2001	v Manchester United			
17.11.2002	v Blackburn Rovers			

Home games shown in red
Fixtures are subject to change
Copyright agreement number IND/CLUB/013

DATE	OPPOSITION	RESULT	SCORERS	★ STAR MAN
24.11.2001	v Sunderland			
1.12.2001	v Derby County			
8.12.2001	v Middlesbrough			
15.12.2001	v Chelsea			
22.12.2001	v Arsenal			
26.12.2001	v Aston Villa			
29.12.2001	v West Ham United			
1.1.2002	v Bolton Wanderers			
12.1.2002	v Arsenal			
19.1.2002	v Southampton			
30.1.2002	v Leicester City			
2.2.2002	v Leeds United			
9.2.2002	v Ipswich Town			
23.2.2002	v Everton			
2.3.2002	v Fulham			
6.3.2002	v Newcastle United			
16.3.2002	v Middlesbrough			
23.3.2002	v Chelsea			
30.3.2002	v Charlton Athletic			
1.4.2002	v Manchester United			
6.4.2002	v Blackburn Rovers			
13.4.2002	v Sunderland			
20.4.2002	v Derby County			
27.4.2002	v Tottenham Hotspur			
11.5.2002	v Ipswich Town			

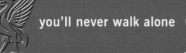
STRIKE**FORCE**

ROBBIE **FOWLER**

D.O.B 9.4.1975	
BIRTHPLACE Liverpool, England	
HEIGHT 1.80m	
TRANSFER FEE Signed as trainee	
LIVERPOOL DEBUT 22 September 1993 vs Fulham	
INTERNATIONAL SIDE England	

"The fans have been magnificent. It's great when they show they have a special place for you in their hearts"

The most prolific and naturally gifted marksman of his generation, Robbie Fowler's status as a Liverpool legend has never been in doubt. Neither has his place at the club, despite numerous misplaced rumours of him leaving Anfield. The striker crushes such gossip by saying, "Other clubs showed an interest in me, but Gérard Houllier was the first person to tell me I wasn't going anywhere. It's so much of a boost when you know the manager still wants you and has faith in you. He's been brilliant."

Following his lethal finish in the Uefa Cup final in Dortmund when he came on as substitute, Robbie said, "I have never complained about being on the bench. I am a local lad and playing for Liverpool means an awful lot to me."

Fowler remains aware of the adoration Reds supporters have for him, saying, "The fans have been magnificent. It feels great when they show they have a special place for you in their hearts."

pictures *steve orino*

IF IT'S GOALSCORERS YOU'RE AFTER THEN LIVERPOOL LEAD THE WAY, WITH FORWARDS WHO STRIKE FEAR INTO THE HEARTS OF DEFENDERS EVERYWHERE...

MICHAEL **OWEN**

D.O.B 14.12.1979	
BIRTHPLACE Chester, England	
HEIGHT 1.75m	
TRANSFER FEE Signed as trainee	
LIVERPOOL DEBUT 6 May 1997 vs Wimbledon	
INTERNATIONAL SIDE England	

"If I can stay fit then I'll score goals. But the most important thing is the success of the team and I'd gladly be in the lower reaches of the scoring charts if we're top of the League table"

In the dying moments of last season's FA Cup final in Cardiff's Millennium Stadium, Michael Owen conjured up two magical goals to snatch the cup from Arsenal and give Liverpool victory in the most dramatic fashion.

Michael's uncanny knack of snatching the headlines with his predatory goalscoring is becoming the stuff of legend. Liverpool's gruelling run of 63 games in season 2000/01 culminated in the Chester-born striker hitting nine goals in his last six matches to help the Reds to cup glory and the mouthwatering prospect of the Champions League.

Last season Michael worked hard to improve his game even further, adding greater movement to his world-beating pace and making him an ideal strike partner for other forwards playing alongside him, be it at club or international level.

Michael remains modest when discussing his ability, saying, "I know what I can do and if I stay fit then I'll score goals. But the most important thing is the success of the team and I'd gladly be in the lower reaches of the scoring charts if we're top of the League table."

STRIKEFORCE

JARI LITMANEN

D.O.B 20.2.1971	
BIRTHPLACE Lahti, Finland	
HEIGHT 1.81m	
TRANSFER FEE Free	
LIVERPOOL DEBUT 10 January 2001 vs Crystal Palace	
PREVIOUS CLUBS Reipas Lahti , HJK Helsinki, MyPa-47, Ajax, Barcelona	
INTERNATIONAL SIDE Finland	

In Amsterdam's Ajax football museum there is a tribute to three of the club's greatest ever players – Johan Cruyff, Marco van Basten and Liverpool's own Jari Litmanen. Jari was idolised at Ajax and it was the Finn's playmaking that helped inspire the Dutch team's European Cup win in 1995.

Gérard Houllier later rushed to secure Jari on a free transfer from Barcelona, knowing he was signing one of the world's best players.

A broken wrist and another injury received while playing for the Reds last term mean Jari has so far shown only teasing glimpses of his talent.

Although a massive star in his homeland of Finland, Jari isn't looking to be singled out at Anfield, saying "It's a matter of how well we perform as a team – the whole team, including players, management and coaching staff."

> **"It's a matter of how well we perform as a team – the whole team, including players, management and coaching staff"**

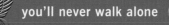
EMILE **HESKEY**

D.O.B 11.1.1978	
BIRTHPLACE Leicester, England	
HEIGHT 1.83m	
TRANSFER FEE £11 million	
LIVERPOOL DEBUT 11 March 2000 vs Sunderland	
INTERNATIONAL SIDE England	

"This is a special club for me and now we have the chance to build on our success. Coming to Liverpool is the best move I could have made. Everyone gets on really well here and the spirit among the lads is first class"

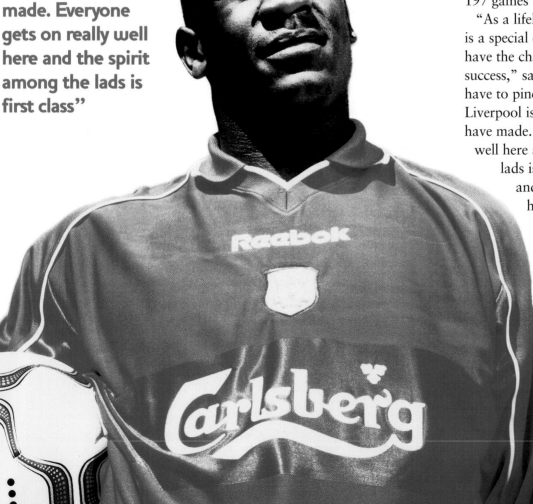

When the Reds splashed out a record-breaking £11m to sign Emile Heskey from Leicester City in March 1999, the new striker was unfairly criticised by some and such a huge transfer fee would have weighed heavily on most young players' shoulders. Not so Emile.

The powerful forward was in electric form throughout last term, tormenting defenders with his strength and tireless energy. But it was his finishing that was one of the season's real high points, registering a total of 23 goals – exactly half as many as he scored in 197 games while at Filbert Street.

"As a lifelong Liverpool fan, this is a special club for me and now we have the chance to build on our success," says Emile. "Sometimes I have to pinch myself – coming to Liverpool is the best move I could have made. Everyone gets on really well here and the spirit among the lads is first class. If we win and I don't score I'm still happy. Obviously I'm delighted when I do get a goal because at the end of the day that's what strikers are judged on, but I feel I can contribute to a good overall team performance as well as my ability to score goals."

THIS IS
**LIVERPOOL
FOOTBALL CLUB
ANFIELD**

3PM KICK-OFF? MORE LIKE CRACK OF DAWN.
IT'S A LONG, LONG MATCHDAY BEHIND THE
SCENES FOR ANFIELD'S UNSUNG HEROES...

GROUND FORCE

pictures *anton want*

Planning for a match starts as soon
the last home game ends and the
priority is always the same – to
make sure that every spectator can
arrive, enjoy the game and leave the
ground in complete safety.

Preparations begin at 10am on
the day before the game, when the
stadium manager has a meeting
with his senior staff. Each person
has responsibility for their own
section, covering such areas as
crowd safety, security, policing, fire
prevention, first aid, stewarding,
turnstile, programmes and catering.

The waste disposal team arrive as early as 7am on a matchday, when final cleaning begins. Catering staff take deliveries of refreshments and the *Matchday Magazine* is also distributed around the ground.

Two hours before kick-off, 25 head stewards give a final briefing to 450 staff and half-an-hour later everyone is in position and ready for the arrival of the first fans.

Anfield has 92 turnstiles and these are all fully staffed as the ground opens 90 minutes before kick-off. At the same time, around 400 other staff who supervise food, drink and *Matchday Magazine* sales are in place. A team of electricians, joiners and plumbers is also on standby in case of emergency.

Anfield has five first aid rooms, two doctors are on duty, as well as

five highly-trained paramedics. Also there to lend a medical hand are 40 St John Ambulance personnel, with three well-equipped ambulances also parked on site. Medical provision at Anfield is first class.

Depending on the fixture, between 45 and 70 Merseyside police officers are on duty inside Anfield, which has its own certified police station and enough room to detain up to 45 people if it were necessary. Incidents are generally both rare and minor though.

The matchday control room is the nerve centre of security and safety in the ground and the police and Anfield's own staff operate it.

A network of closed circuit TV cameras dotted around the stadium can zoom in to take a look at the stands and concourses to ensure

that all regulations are being obeyed by both sets of supporters.

A team of 40 safety stewards continually patrol the public areas behind the stands within the ground to check everything is okay before, during and after the game.

After 70 minutes of play, the main exit points around the ground are opened by staff sitting in the match control room, ready for the mass exodus by supporters which takes place when the game is over.

It's possible in fact to evacuate everybody from the ground in as little as eight minutes, and even more quickly in specific areas of the stadium if a serious incident occurs while the match is in progress.

Once the game is over, the entire matchday operation has to be reversed and the whole stadium is then cleaned for a couple of hours.

The closing down procedure also begins, including a very thorough search to ensure that there are no spectators locked inside.

An hour and a half after the final whistle has been blown the ground is empty, apart from people still in the hospitality lounges, enjoying something to eat and drink.

By 7pm, 12 hours after all the hard work first began, the ground is now empty and another day in the life of Anfield is just about over. Until the next home game, that is.

Around 1,200 unsung heroes have helped make everything run smoothly and whatever their jobs, whether they work on safety, security, catering or stewarding, they are all very important people in the overall management and safety of Anfield on a matchday.

WHEN SUNDAY 25 FEB 2001
WHERE MILLENNIUM STADIUM
SCORE BIRMINGHAM CITY 4
LIVERPOOL 5 (after penalties)

ROBBIE SCORES WITH A STUNNING LONG-RANGER, BUT CITY EQUALISE AND FOLLOWING EXTRA TIME IT GOES TO PENALTIES. JAMIE CARRAGHER SCORES OUR FIFTH AND, AFTER HEROICS FROM SANDER, LIVERPOOL ARE LEAGUE CUP WINNERS FOR A RECORD SIXTH TIME.

A major English cup final takes place outside England for the very first time and Liverpool are victors.

The match perhaps fails to live up to the high expectations, apart from Robbie's amazing goal of course, as Fowler gives the Reds the lead on the half-hour with a superb looping volley worthy of any cup final.

With three minutes of time added on after 90 minutes, Stephane Henchoz brings down Martin O'Connor and referee David Elleray awards a penalty. Darren Purse converts and the game goes into extra time. Liverpool take charge, but neither side is able to break the deadlock. Penalties are to decide it.

Liverpool miss their fourth attempt, but after Jamie Carragher successfully converts the sixth, it's sudden death. Having already saved one, Sander gets his hands to another and the Reds lift the trophy.

Robbie Fowler is flying high after giving Liverpool the lead on the half-hour

Liverpool show that when it comes to a penalty shoot-out, they're spot-on...

McALLISTER 1-0

Gary fires it top-right...

BARMBY 2-1

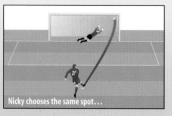

Nicky chooses the same spot...

ZIEGE 3-1

Christian calmly hits it top-left...

WORTHINGTON CUP FINAL

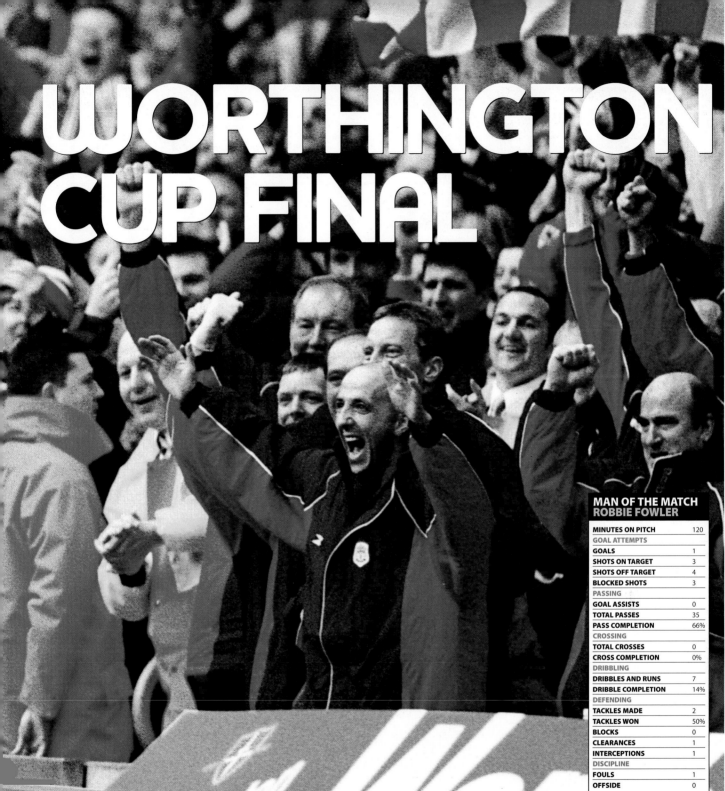

MAN OF THE MATCH ROBBIE FOWLER	
MINUTES ON PITCH	120
GOAL ATTEMPTS	
GOALS	1
SHOTS ON TARGET	3
SHOTS OFF TARGET	4
BLOCKED SHOTS	3
PASSING	
GOAL ASSISTS	0
TOTAL PASSES	35
PASS COMPLETION	66%
CROSSING	
TOTAL CROSSES	0
CROSS COMPLETION	0%
DRIBBLING	
DRIBBLES AND RUNS	7
DRIBBLE COMPLETION	14%
DEFENDING	
TACKLES MADE	2
TACKLES WON	50%
BLOCKS	0
CLEARANCES	1
INTERCEPTIONS	1
DISCIPLINE	
FOULS	1
OFFSIDE	0

picture mark leech illustrations roy cooper

HAMANN 3-2	FOWLER 4-3	CARRAGHER 5-4	WESTERVELD SAVES

Straight at the keeper for Didi...

Robbie's left foot fires the ball top-right...

Jamie decides to go top-right as well...

Sander saves City's sixth – game over

MILESTONES

FROM LOCAL AMATEURS TO TREBLE-WINNING HEROES, THE REDS HAVE A UNIQUE AND GLORIOUS HISTORY…

IN THE BEGINNING…

- St Domingo's Football Club forms in Liverpool in 1878.
- Name changes to Everton FC in 1879, play on Stanley Park.
- Team moves to its current Anfield Road site in 1884.
- Everton beat Earlstown 5-0 in the first game at Anfield on 28 September 1884 and the club thrives for the next eight years. Game turns professional in 1885.
- Anfield begins to take shape. Everton become a founding member of the Football League in 1888 and now play games all over the country. Behind the scenes all is not well though.

THE BIRTH OF LIVERPOOL FC

- There is bitter disagreement at the club over ground rent in 1892. The majority of club directors decide to leave to form a new club, also called Everton.
- The original club changes its name to Liverpool Association Football Club in May 1892 and John McKenna is club manager.
- Liverpool's first game at Anfield is against Rotherham Town on 1 September 1892. The team has no English players, shirts are blue and white and Liverpool win 7-1.
- Attendances at Anfield are poor to begin with, but Liverpool win their league in that first season.

The view from outside Anfield on matchday in the early 1900s

FIRST DIVISION CHAMPIONS

- September 1893 – Liverpool join Division Two.
- In 1893/94 they're promoted to Division One, but are relegated the next season. W.E. Barclay joins McKenna as manager.
- Liverpool storm to promotion in 1895/96 and stay in the top flight for eight years. Tom Watson becomes manager in 1896.
- In 1898/99 'the Anfielders' replace their old blue and white quartered jersey with a red one.
- Liverpool win the First Division for the first time in 1900/01 and do the same again in 1905/06, having won the Division Two the season before. A new stand is erected at the Anfield Road end

in 1903 and the Kop and Kemlyn Road stands begin to take shape in 1906.

PRE-WORLD WAR II

- Liverpool reach their first FA Cup final in 1914, but Burnley win the match 1-0 at Crystal Palace. Britain goes to war and league football is suspended in 1915.
- David Ashworth becomes manager in 1920, Liverpool win First Division titles in 1921/22 and 1922/23. Matt McQueen becomes manager in 1923, then George Patterson in 1928. A roof is then built over the Kop.
- George Kay takes over as manager in 1936. Football is again suspended with the outbreak of World War II in 1939 and regional leagues are established.

THE 1940s AND 50s

- The Reds win their fifth title in 1946/47.
- Liverpool lose the 1950 FA Cup final to Arsenal 2-0 at Wembley. George Kay retires in 1951 and is replaced by Don Welsh. Liverpool are relegated to Division Two in 1953/54 after 50 years in the top-flight, despite maintaining gates in excess of 60,000 at Anfield.
- In 1956 Don Welsh becomes the first Liverpool manager to be sacked. Phil Taylor, former player and captain of the 1950 FA Cup final team, takes over.
- Liverpool struggle on and Phil Taylor finally leaves the club, replaced in 1959 as manager by the legendary Bill Shankly.

The official Wembley matchday programme from when the Reds first won the FA Cup in 1965

THE SWINGING 60s

- Liverpool win the Second Division in 1961/62 and are promoted. Anfield is famous for the way the Liverpool fans sing about their team.
- Liverpool win the First Division title in 1963/64. In October 1963, the Kop adopts *You'll Never Walk Alone* as the club's anthem.
- At Shankly's insistence, Liverpool change to an all-red kit. In 1965 the Reds beat Leeds 2-1 to win the FA Cup for the first time.
- Liverpool win Division One in 1965/66. Three players – Gerry Byrne, Ian Callaghan and Roger Hunt – get the call-up for England's World Cup-winning squad.

A team photo from 1949 when George Kay (far right) was manager

THE CLUB BADGE

Liverpool's crest is made up of different parts that tell of important events from the club's long and proud history.

The Liver Bird is not a real creature – it is a mythical cross between an eagle and a cormorant. When Liverpool was granted the status of city by King John in 1207 the Liver Bird was first used as a seal or official stamp. Ever since, the Liver Bird has become the traditional symbol of the City of Liverpool and it is therefore incorporated in the badge of the club most closely associated with the city.

You'll Never Walk Alone has been associated with Liverpool since October 1963. Fans on the Kop sang it before games when local group Gerry and the Pacemakers' version was number one in the charts. Shortly afterwards the song was adopted as the official club anthem and it is still sung at Anfield by fans before and during games.

The Shankly Gates can be seen at the entrance to the Main Stand at Anfield. They were built to commemorate legendary manager Bill Shankly's massive contribution to Liverpool FC. The year of the club's formation, 1892, is also shown.

The flames honour the memories of the 96 Liverpool supporters who lost their lives at Hillsborough in 1989.

Rome 1984: Liverpool celebrate a fourth European Cup success

THE SUPERB 70s
- Shankly's men lift the Uefa Cup in 1972/73 and also win the club's eighth First Division title.
- Liverpool beat Newcastle 3-0 in the 1973/74 FA Cup final. In July 1974 Bill Shankly unexpectedly retires as Liverpool manager. Bob Paisley reluctantly takes charge.
- Paisley guides Liverpool to the League title and another Uefa Cup final triumph in 1975/76.
- The Reds win the European Cup for the first time in 1976/77 and another League title – their tenth.
- Dalglish scores as the Reds retain the European Cup at Wembley in May 1978. More league titles in 1978/79 and 1979/80 make it 12.

THE GLORIOUS 80s
- In 1980/81 the Reds finally lift the League Cup for the first time.
- Liverpool win the European Cup for the third time in May 1981, beating Real Madrid 1-0 in Paris.
- 1981/82 – Liverpool win a 13th title and the League Cup again.
- The Reds make it 14 titles in 1982/83 and win the League Cup once more. Bob Paisley retires.
- Joe Fagan takes over in 1983/84 and guides the Reds to a 15th championship and League Cup glory for a record fourth time. Liverpool win the European Cup for the fourth time, beating Roma in Rome on penalties.

- Liverpool's 1985 European Cup final appearance ends in tragedy at Heysel Stadium in Brussels with the deaths of 39 Juventus fans. Juve win the game 1-0, but the result is academic.
- Fagan retires and Kenny Dalglish becomes player/manager for the 1985/86 season. The Reds win the League and the double by beating Everton 3-1 in a thrilling FA Cup final.
- Liverpool make it 17 League championships in 1987/88.
- On 15 April 1989, 96 Liverpool supporters are tragically crushed to death at Hillsborough during the FA Cup semi-final game against Nottingham Forest.
- Liverpool go on to beat Everton in an emotional Wembley final.

THE LEAN 90s
- A record-breaking 18th title in May 1990. Dalglish resigns 1991.

- Souness takes over and the Reds win the FA Cup in 1992.
- Roy Evans takes over in 1993/94.
- The Kop becomes all-seater in 1994 and Liverpool win the Coca-Cola Cup in 1995.
- In 1998 Gérard Houllier becomes joint manager. The experimental partnership fails and Roy Evans leaves Anfield in December.

THE FUTURE...
- 2000/01 – Houllier guides the Reds to an historic cup treble and into the Champions League. Liverpool are back.

CLUB HONOURS

League Champions
1900/01 1905/06 1921/22 1922/23 1946/47 1963/64 1965/66 1972/73 1975/76 1976/77 1978/79 1979/80 1981/82 1982/83 1983/84 1985/86 1987/88 1989/90
European Cup winners
1976/77 1977/78 1980/81 1983/84
European Super Cup winners 1977
Uefa Cup winners 1972/73 1975/76 2000/01
FA Cup winners
1964/65 1973/74 1985/86 1988/89 1991/92 2000/01
League/Coca-Cola/Worthington Cup winners
1980/81 1994/95 2000/01
Milk Cup winners
1981/82 1982/83 1983/84

Anfield of today is one of the finest football grounds in Europe

2000/01 SEASON REVIEW

LAST SEASON WILL GO DOWN AS ONE OF THE REDS' BEST EVER. TIME THEN TO RELIVE THE GAMES AND GOALS ON THAT ROAD TO AN HISTORIC TREBLE AND CHAMPIONS LEAGUE QUALIFICATION...

[H] = HOME   [A] = AWAY

AUGUST 2000

19 BRADFORD CITY [H]
A brilliant strike from Emile earns a 1-0 Liverpool victory as new signings Markus Babbel and Nick Barmby make their Red debuts.

21 ARSENAL [A]
Referee Graham Poll sends off Gary Mac and Didi Hamann, along with the Gunners' Patrick Vieira as the Reds go down 2-0.

26 SOUTHAMPTON [A]
Michael scores two, Sami heads in a third, but unbelievably the Saints get three back to earn a draw.

GOALS 4
LEAGUE POSITION 12

Emile opened his account for the season with an impressive strike against Bradford City at Anfield

SEPTEMBER 2000

6 ASTON VILLA [H]
A spectacular first-half hat-trick by an in-form Michael Owen seals a memorable 3-1 victory over the Villans at Anfield.

9 MANCHESTER CITY [H]
A close game in which Christian Ziege makes his Liverpool debut. Michael gives the Reds the lead and then Didi makes it two. Weah gets one back and a Horlock penalty ties the game with 10 minutes to go. From the kick-off Didi is there again to win it 3-2.

14 RAPID BUCHAREST [A]
A tricky Uefa Cup first round tie in Romania, but Nick scores a cracker on the half-hour and Liverpool hold out. Robbie comes on as substitute for his first appearance of the season and Bernard Diomède makes his debut.

17 WEST HAM [A]
Steven Gerrard spectacularly puts Liverpool 1-0 up early on, but the Reds are unfortunate and a second-half Paolo Di Canio penalty sees the points shared in a hard-fought encounter.

23 SUNDERLAND [H]
Kevin Phillips gives the Black Cats an early lead, but Michael is there with a tremendous headed equaliser. Robbie makes a second-half appearance but it ends 1-1.

28 RAPID BUCHAREST [H]
Djimi Traore keeps his place at left back and Patrik Berger returns from injury. The game ends 0-0 but it doesn't matter – Liverpool are through to the second round.

GOALS 9
LEAGUE POSITION 4

OCTOBER 2000

1 CHELSEA [A]
An off day for the Reds as they crash 3-0 at Stamford Bridge.

15 DERBY COUNTY [A]
Liverpool bounce back with an exceptional 4-0 win – a fabulous Emile hat-trick and a memorable long-ranger from Patrik. Gary Mac makes a welcome return, but Michael receives a severe head injury which needs six stitches.

21 LEICESTER CITY [H]
Another impressive Liverpool display and a 1-0 victory as Emile scores against his old club.

26 SLOVAN LIBEREC [H]
Emile's on target again, but leaves it until the 88th minute to give the Reds a valuable 1-0 lead to take to the second leg in the Czech Republic.

Patrik scores Liverpool's third and leaves the Toffees feeling blue

29 EVERTON [H]
Nick scores the Reds' first against his old club, Emile gets another and Paddy settles it from the spot as Liverpool romp it 3-1 in the pouring rain.

GOALS 9
LEAGUE POSITION 3

NOVEMBER 2000

1 CHELSEA [H]
Danny nets with a fantastic strike, Zola gets one back, but Robbie wraps it up in extra time and it ends 2-1 in the Worthies Cup.

4 LEEDS UNITED [A]
Sami, Christian and Vlad all score but Liverpool still lose 4-3. Mark Viduka scores all four for Leeds.

9 SLOVAN LIBEREC [A]
Nick, Emile and Michael are all on target as the Reds win 3-2 and go through to the Uefa Cup third round.

12 COVENTRY CITY [H]
Liverpool run out 4-1 winners at Anfield with strikes by Gary Mac, Stevie G and two from Emile.

19 TOTTENHAM HOTSPUR [A]
Robbie scores a belter but the Reds still go down 2-1.

23 OLYMPIAKOS [A]
It's a draw in Greece, but the Reds get two important away goals thanks to Nick and Stevie G.

26 NEWCASTLE UNITED [A]
Emile gets one but Liverpool concede two and it's another away defeat in the League.

29 STOKE CITY [A]
The Reds hammer the Potters 8-0 in the Worthington Cup. Robbie gets three, Christian, Markus, Vlad, Sami and Danny also get on the scoresheet.

GOALS 24
LEAGUE POSITION 5

Hat-trick hero Robbie Fowler is congratulated in the Worthington Cup demolition of Stoke City

DECEMBER 2000

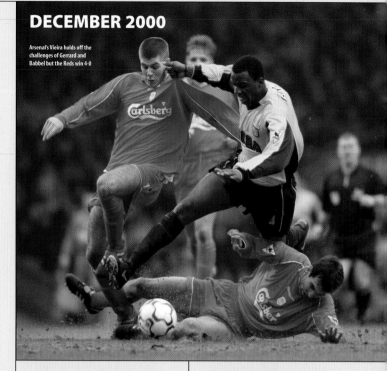

Arsenal's Vieira holds off the challenges of Gerrard and Babbel but the Reds win 4-0

2 CHARLTON ATHLETIC [H]
Strikes from Markus and Emile, plus an Addicks own goal, help Liverpool to a 3-0 win.

7 OLYMPIAKOS [H]
Emile and Nick give the Reds a 2-0 win over the Greeks and it's into round four of the Uefa Cup.

10 IPSWICH TOWN [H]
The Tractor Boys win 1-0, but at least Igor Biscan makes an impressive home debut.

13 FULHAM [H]
Michael, Vlad and Nick score three in extra time and we're into the Worthington Cup semi-finals.

17 MANCHESTER UNITED [A]
Liverpool dominate at Old Trafford and come away with a memorable 1-0 victory courtesy of a superb long-range free-kick from Danny Murphy.

23 ARSENAL [H]
The Gunners are out-gunned 4-0, with goals from Robbie, Michael, Stevie G and Nick.

26 MIDDLESBROUGH [A]
Boxing Day blues as we go down 1-0 to the Premiership strugglers.

GOALS 13
LEAGUE POSITION 6

JANUARY 2001

1 SOUTHAMPTON [H]
A 2-1 victory for Liverpool with goals by Markus and Stevie G.

6 ROTHERHAM UNITED [H]
Two goals by Emile and one by Didi sink the Millers as the Reds' FA Cup campaign kicks off.

10 CRYSTAL PALACE [A]
Liverpool lose 2-1 in the first leg of the Worthies semi-final.

13 ASTON VILLA [A]
A 3-0 win, with two from Danny and one from Stevie G.

20 MIDDLESBROUGH [H]
Liverpool fail to break down Boro in a drab, goalless affair.

24 CRYSTAL PALACE [H]
The Reds smash five past the First Division Eagles with no reply.

27 LEEDS UNITED [A]
Round four of the FA Cup. The Reds win 2-0, with late goals from substitutes Emile and Nick.

31 MANCHESTER CITY [A]
Emile scores, but it ends honours even at Maine Road.

GOALS 17
LEAGUE POSITION 4

FEBRUARY 2001

3 WEST HAM UNITED [H]
Two from Robbie and one from Vlad sink the Hammers 3-0.

10 SUNDERLAND [A]
We share the points again, but Jari Litmanen opens his account for Liverpool from the spot.

15 ROMA [A]
An historic 2-0 victory in Italy thanks to a second-half double strike from Michael Owen.

18 MANCHESTER CITY [H]
Liverpool are through to the FA Cup quarter-final thanks to a 4-2 victory, with goals from Markus, Vlad, Emile and Jari.

22 ROMA [H]
The Italians score one but the Reds go through on a special tribute night at Anfield in honour of former manager Bob Paisley.

25 BIRMINGHAM CITY [A]
Robbie hits a cracker, the Blues equalise, but after penalties Liverpool are victorious in the Worthington Cup final at Cardiff.

GOALS 11
LEAGUE POSITION 4

Liverpool lift the League Cup for the sixth time thanks to Sander's super saves

MARCH 2001

3 LEICESTER CITY [A]
It's back down to earth in the Premiership and no points at Filbert Street as we lose 2-0.

8 PORTO [A]
A solid performance earns the Reds a goalless draw in the first leg of the Uefa Cup quarter-final.

11 TRANMERE ROVERS [A]
A spirited display by Rovers, but in the end Liverpool have too much class and run out 4-2 winners, with goals from Danny, Michael, Stevie G and Robbie.

15 PORTO [H]
Danny and Michael are both on song and with a 2-0 scoreline Liverpool book their place in the Uefa Cup semi-finals.

18 DERBY COUNTY [H]
The Rams go ahead but the Reds fight back for a 1-1 draw, thanks once again to Michael.

31 MANCHESTER UNITED [H]
Outplayed, outclassed, outwitted. Stevie G opens the scoring with another long-ranger, and Robbie knocks in another before half time. A superb display gives the Reds a League double over United – the first for 22 seasons.

GOALS 9
LEAGUE POSITION 4

APRIL 2001

5 BARCELONA [A]
A superb defensive display in front of 90,000 at the Nou Camp. It ends goalless, giving the Reds a great chance for the second leg of the Uefa Cup semi at Anfield.

The flags are out for the FA Cup semi-final at Villa Park

8 WYCOMBE WANDERERS [A]
A header from Emile and a stunning free-kick from Robbie at Villa Park book Liverpool's return to Cardiff and a place in the FA Cup final against Arsenal.

10 IPSWICH TOWN [A]
Emile puts the Reds ahead in the second half, but Ipswich force a 1-1 draw at Portman Road.

13 LEEDS UNITED [H]
Leeds are 2-0 up by half time as tiredness looks to have caught up with the Reds. A strike by Stevie G isn't enough and it ends 2-1.

16 EVERTON [A]
Liverpool take the lead twice, but the Blues pull back. Then Gary Mac's 44-yard free-kick, almost the last kick of the game, secures the points for the Reds.

19 BARCELONA [A]
Gary Mac scores from the spot before half time and the Reds hang on for a memorable 1-0 victory and a place in the Uefa Cup final in Dortmund.

22 TOTTENHAM HOTSPUR [H]
Emile scores an early one, Spurs equalise, but Gary Mac is on song again from the spot and Robbie wraps it up as it ends 3-1.

28 COVENTRY CITY [A]
The Reds leave it late, but Sami and Gary Mac give Liverpool a well-earned 2-0 away victory.

GOALS 13
LEAGUE POSITION 5

MAY 2001

1 BRADFORD CITY [A]
Two second-half goals from Michael and Gary Mac give the Reds another valuable away win as they push for a Champions League spot.

5 NEWCASTLE UNITED [H]
A superb hat-trick from Michael sinks the Magpies at Anfield.

8 CHELSEA [H]
Michael again is on form to net twice but the game ends in a draw as Jimmy Floyd Hasselbaink replies with two for the Blues.

12 ARSENAL [A]
Michael dashes the Gunners' hopes with two magnificent late strikes to bring the FA Cup back to Anfield for the sixth time. That makes it two out of two cup final successes and the historic treble is still very much on.

16 ALAVES [A]
It's a close thing and definitely not for the faint-hearted, but the Reds finally win 5-4 after a golden goal deep into extra time. One of the most exciting European finals ever, and Liverpool achieve a famous treble. The celebrations must wait a while longer though.

19 CHARLTON ATHLETIC [A]
Liverpool need victory to ensure Champions League football next season and it doesn't look too good in the first half as the Addicks run the show. After the break though, the Reds step up a gear and goals from Robbie (2), Michael and Danny finally bring victory and with it a precious Champions League entry.

GOALS 19
LEAGUE POSITION 3

MIDDLEMEN

> "It means the world to me to play for this club. I'd sign for the rest of my career if Liverpool want me to"

STEVEN **GERRARD**
D.O.B 30.5.1980
BIRTHPLACE Liverpool, England
HEIGHT 1.83m
TRANSFER FEE Signed as trainee
LIVERPOOL DEBUT 29 November 1998 vs Blackburn Rovers
INTERNATIONAL SIDE England

GARY **McALLISTER**
D.O.B 25.12.1964
BIRTHPLACE Motherwell, Scotland
HEIGHT 1.81m
TRANSFER FEE Free
LIVERPOOL DEBUT 19 August 2000 vs Bradford City
PREVIOUS CLUBS Motherwell, Leicester City, Leeds United, Coventry City
INTERNATIONAL SIDE Scotland

Steven Gerrard possesses all the qualities needed by the classic modern-day midfielder: strength, speed, skill, courage, as well as being an excellent passer of the ball.

Crowned as Liverpool's player of the season last term, Stevie G produced some of the most inspired performances seen in midfield at Anfield since former skipper Graeme Souness' heyday. His stunning goals (remember that long-range effort against Manchester United at Anfield?) and all-action performances were key factors in Liverpool's record-breaking campaign.

"I used to be a Liverpool fan watching the open-top parades and now I'm a part of that success," says Steven, adding, "It means the world to me to play for this club. I would sign for the rest of my career if Liverpool want me to."

Gary McAllister may feel unlucky not to have been voted the PFA player of the season last term – even at the age of 36. His world-class consistency in his first season with the Reds helped them to win some of their most demanding fixtures.

The inspirational Scot also scored five vital goals in five games, including the winning penalty against Barcelona in the Uefa Cup semi-final second leg and superb free-kicks against Everton and his former club Coventry.

Reflecting on life with the Reds, Gary says, "I was delighted to join the club and I'm loving every second of it. I've always been an admirer of the way Liverpool have tried to play football and it's great to be part of that now."

picture *anthony crolla*

THE TOUGH-TACKLING BALL WINNERS, THE PLAYMAKERS, THE DEAD-BALL SPECIALISTS AND THE GOALSCORERS. WE WELCOME YOU TO THE REDS' ALL-STAR MIDFIELD...

DIETMAR **HAMANN**

D.O.B	27.8.1973
BIRTHPLACE	Waldsasson, Germany
HEIGHT	1.89m
TRANSFER FEE	£8 million
LIVERPOOL DEBUT	17 August 1999 vs Sheffield Wednesday
PREVIOUS CLUBS	Bayern Munich, Newcastle United
INTERNATIONAL SIDE	Germany

DANNY **MURPHY**

D.O.B	18.3.1977
BIRTHPLACE	Chester, England
HEIGHT	1.74m
TRANSFER FEE	£2 million
LIVERPOOL DEBUT	9 August 1998 vs Wimbledon
PREVIOUS CLUBS	Crewe Alexandra
INTERNATIONAL SIDE	England

Dietmar Hamann is Liverpool's tireless midfield maestro, the man who breaks up attack after attack before revving up the Red engine and slicing through opposition defences with his pinpoint passes.

Last season Didi began to show glimpses of the magic that persuaded the Liverpool boss to splash out £8m to sign him from Newcastle United in July 1999. Reds fans will remember his two stunning match-winning goals against Manchester City at the start of the 2000/01 Premiership campaign, but it was against Roma in the fourth round of last season's Uefa Cup that he really sparkled, dominating the middle of the park over both legs.

"I think we're on our way to bringing the glory days back here," says Dietmar, "and I want to be a major part of that."

Danny Murphy's a real favourite with Reds fans and not just because it was his superb free-kick that ended a ten-year 'hoodoo' against Manchester United at Old Trafford in December last season.

Roy Evans brought Danny to Anfield in July 1997, although he didn't feature regularly for the Reds until the 1999/00 season, when he scored six goals. Last season Danny weighed in with another 10 goals and now stands on the verge of a senior England call-up.

"My priority has always been Liverpool though," explains Danny. "They're the club I supported as a kid and to win things with them is like a dream."

> **"Liverpool are the club that I supported as a kid and to win things with them is like a dream"**

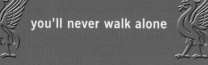
MIDDLEMEN

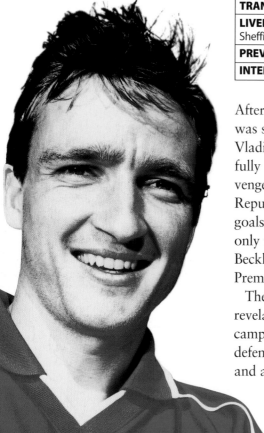

"I always knew that signing for this club would be a good move for me"

VLADIMIR **SMICER**
D.O.B 24.5.1973
BIRTHPLACE Decin, Czech Republic
HEIGHT 1.77m
TRANSFER FEE £4.2 million
LIVERPOOL DEBUT 17 August 1999 vs Sheffield Wednesday
PREVIOUS CLUBS Slavia Prague, Lens
INTERNATIONAL SIDE Czech Republic

NICK **BARMBY**
D.O.B 11.2.1974
BIRTHPLACE Hull, England
HEIGHT 1.69m
TRANSFER FEE £6 million
LIVERPOOL DEBUT 19 August 2000 vs Bradford City
PREVIOUS CLUBS Tottenham Hotspur, Middlesbrough, Everton
INTERNATIONAL SIDE England

After a first term for Liverpool that was so cruelly ravaged by injury, Vladimir Smicer's confidence is now fully restored. Returning with a vengeance last season, the Czech Republic international scored seven goals in total and finished second only to Manchester United's David Beckham for assists-per-game in Premiership matches.

The tricky midfielder was a revelation throughout the 2000/01 campaign, tormenting opposing defences with his speedy dribbling and an array of flicks and tricks.

Vlad has settled in well at Liverpool and he's a firm favourite with the fans. He says, "I always knew signing for this club would be a good move for me. I'm really happy training every day and playing at Anfield is a great experience. If you can't enjoy yourself here then there must be something wrong."

It takes a very strong individual to make the move across Stanley Park from Everton to Liverpool, but Nick Barmby has done just that and the Reds have reaped the rewards.

Nick immediately added a new dimension to Liverpool's midfield with his elusive running and ability to link up with the front players. And he didn't have to wait long to score his first League goal for the club, a header in the Merseyside derby at Anfield last October.

After completing the season with a total of eight goals, the boyhood Red says he's pleased to be a part of Gérard Houllier's treble-winning side. "I was brought up watching some of the best footballers around and it's amazing to think I'm following in their footsteps. I love life at Liverpool. I'm happy here."

IGOR **BISCAN**

D.O.B	4.5.1978
BIRTHPLACE	Zagreb, Croatia
HEIGHT	1.89m
TRANSFER FEE	£5.5 million
LIVERPOOL DEBUT	10 December 2000 vs Ipswich Town
PREVIOUS CLUBS	Samobor, Dinamo Zagreb
INTERNATIONAL SIDE	Croatia

PATRIK **BERGER**

D.O.B	10.11.1973
BIRTHPLACE	Prague, Czech Republic
HEIGHT	1.86m
TRANSFER FEE	£3.2 million
LIVERPOOL DEBUT	7 September 1996 vs Southampton
INTERNATIONAL SIDE	Czech Republic

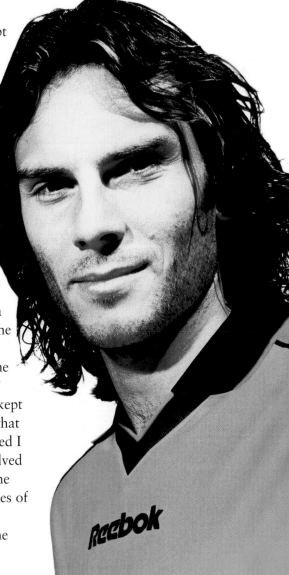

> "Throughout my time on the sidelines I kept telling myself that when I returned I could be involved in some of the biggest games of my footballing career"

Liverpool's multicultural side was spiced up even further in December 2000 when Gérard Houllier signed one of Europe's finest youngsters from Dinamo Zagreb, seeing off competition from Barcelona, Juventus and AC Milan.

Igor was already a Croatia international and captain of Zagreb at only 22 years of age when the Reds manager moved for him.

Next season Igor will be looking to add to the single goal he scored for Liverpool last term, a superb solo run and strike against Crystal Palace in the Worthington Cup semi-final second leg victory at Anfield.

Igor remembers one of the first times he experienced the overwhelming Anfield atmosphere: "Just before a game last season I phoned my mum and then *You'll Never Walk Alone* played over the speakers. It gave me tingles down my spine."

A knee injury sustained in the opening game of last season kept Patrik Berger out of action for two months. Then his comeback was cut short by a flare-up of the problem. This second injury spell meant Liverpool would be frustratingly deprived of the midfielder for another five months.

Finally fit again, Paddy returned to face Manchester United in the fantastic 2-0 win at Anfield and also made a telling contribution in the Uefa Cup final.

"Throughout my time on the sidelines," says Paddy, "I kept telling myself that when I returned I could beinvolved in some of the biggest games of my career." How right he was.

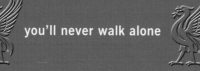
MIDDLEMEN

JAMIE **REDKNAPP**

D.O.B 25.6.1973	
BIRTHPLACE Barton-on-Sea, England	
HEIGHT 1.78m	
TRANSFER FEE £350,000	
LIVERPOOL DEBUT 23 October 1991 vs Auxerre	
PREVIOUS CLUBS Bournemouth	
INTERNATIONAL SIDE England	

BERNARD **DIOMEDE**

D.O.B 23.1.1974	
BIRTHPLACE Saint-Doulchard, France	
HEIGHT 1.64m	
TRANSFER FEE £3 million	
LIVERPOOL DEBUT 14 September 2000 vs Rapid Bucharest	
PREVIOUS CLUBS Auxerre	
INTERNATIONAL SIDE France	

"There's a grand plan in place at Anfield and I want to be part of it"

At the start of the 1999/2000 season Jamie Redknapp was named Liverpool captain, but a knee injury has forced him to sit out most of Liverpool's crusade ever since.

The longest-serving player currently on the club's books, Jamie is the engine of the Reds' midfield, blessed with an exceptional passing ability and a thunderous shot.

Expected to return for the start of season 2001/02, Jamie's raring to join up with his team-mates again. "The club have been brilliant to me and the lads have gone out of their way to keep me a part of things. The team spirit and camaraderie here have been a huge help to me."

Bernard Diomède has become one of Anfield's forgotten men as the lightning-quick winger's first season was interrupted by niggling injuries.

Having made an impressive Reds debut in the 1-0 Uefa Cup win over Rapid Bucharest last September, Bernard's first-team appearances were then cut short after he received his first injury blow.

A World Cup winner with France, the diminutive international has since featured heavily in the reserves and become a major goal-scoring threat.

Without doubt Bernard is a class act and he was quick to state his intentions to stay and fight for his place in the team, saying, "There's a grand plan in place at Anfield and I want to be part of it."

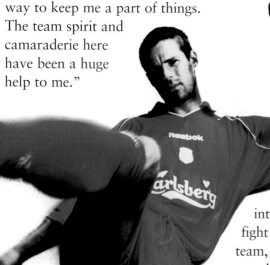

LIVERPOOL WORDSEARCH

HOW EAGLE-EYED ARE YOU WHEN IT COMES TO SPOTTING A LIVERPOOL PLAYER'S NAME? FILL IN THE BLANKS SHOWN ON THE RIGHT AND THEN SEE IF YOU CAN FIND THE MISSING WORDS IN THE GRID BELOW

SEE PAGE 60 FOR ANSWERS

1   _Sander_ Westerveld
2   Stephane _Henchoz_
3   _Robbie_ Fowler
4   Sami _Hyypia_
5   _Michael_ Owen
6   Nick _Barmby_
7   _Danny_ Murphy
8   Markus _Babbel_
9   _Jamie_ Carragher
10 Patrik _Berger_

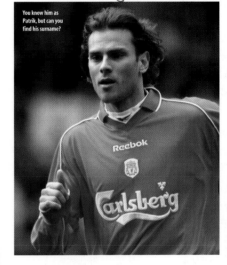

You know him as Patrik, but can you find his surname?

A	I	P	Y	Y	H	Z	B	V	I	G	N	A	L	X
A	K	C	W	B	E	Q	L	M	E	S	M	D	Q	O
J	S	T	D	A	N	N	Y	B	X	L	S	I	Y	U
A	H	D	W	Q	C	K	E	D	J	A	R	I	B	V
M	Z	A	B	L	H	I	K	W	A	E	E	F	M	Q
I	G	R	B	M	O	K	S	T	M	L	D	K	R	P
E	V	E	X	S	Z	H	E	Z	I	S	N	J	A	C
M	Z	T	Q	J	T	N	H	Y	E	X	A	L	B	H
I	N	S	W	X	R	K	D	V	X	D	S	H	G	R
C	E	I	Z	B	A	B	B	E	L	Q	C	H	S	I
H	V	L	N	S	O	R	J	Z	K	C	V	A	Q	S
A	E	L	A	H	R	O	B	B	I	E	T	M	W	T
E	T	A	A	Q	E	Z	P	S	G	T	X	A	V	I
L	S	C	K	H	X	L	M	R	O	A	W	N	T	A
F	P	M	E	B	E	R	G	E	R	K	E	N	M	N

11 Emile _Heskey_
12 _Steven_ ~~Step!~~ Gerrard
13 Dietmar _Hamann_
14 _Igor_ Biscan
15 Gary _McAllister_
16 _Jamie_ Redknapp
17 Gregory _Vignal_
18 _Jari_ Litmanen
19 Djimi _Traore_
20 _Christian_ Ziege

FA CUP

LIVERPOOL HAVE ANOTHER APPOINTMENT IN CARDIFF, TAKING ON ARSENAL IN THE 2001 FA CUP FINAL. THE ONLY THING HOTTER THAN THE BOILING AFTERNOON SUNSHINE IS THE FORM OF LIVERPOOL'S SUPERSTAR STRIKER MICHAEL OWEN.

It was one of the most famous comebacks ever witnessed in a cup final. With just over 15 minutes to go, Liverpool are 1-0 down and the dream of an historic cup treble looks close to being dashed.

Cue a sensational volley from Michael Owen to equalise. Five minutes later Michael runs on to a long Patrik Berger pass, goes past two defenders and dramatically slots the ball home. Liverpool win the FA Cup for the sixth time in a game that will be remembered as the 'Michael Owen cup final'.

"If anyone had told me I would score two goals in 10 minutes in an FA Cup final I would never have believed them," said Michael after the game. "It was the first senior cup final I have played in and, however long I go on to play for, I doubt whether anything will ever match it for drama and excitement. I don't think I've ever been more elated at the end of a match."

Star man Michael Owen celebrates Liverpool's equaliser, unaware he's about to clinch the cup for the Reds

CUP FINAL TIMELINE FIRST HALF

4 5 6 7 8 9 **10** 11 12 13 14 15 16 **17** 18 19 20 21 22 23 24 25 26 27 28

Emile Heskey uses all his strength to get past Arsenal skipper Tony Adams and fellow defender Lee Dixon. He runs through on goal but is stopped in his tracks when he runs into Gilles Grimandi in the Gunners' penalty box. Play is waved on.

Arsenal striker Thierry Henry has his appeal for a penalty turned down by referee Steve Dunn as his shot is deflected behind and away from Liverpool's open goal by Stephane Henchoz's elbow. Instead Liverpool are awarded a goal kick.

Michael goes past Arsenal skipper Tony Adams to score the winner

FINAL

MAN OF THE MATCH
MICHAEL OWEN

MINUTES ON PITCH	90
GOAL ATTEMPTS	
GOALS	2
SHOTS ON TARGET	2
SHOTS OFF TARGET	0
BLOCKED SHOTS	1
PASSING	
GOAL ASSISTS	0
TOTAL PASSES	10
PASS COMPLETION	80%
CROSSING	
TOTAL CROSSES	2
CROSS COMPLETION	0%
DRIBBLING	
DRIBBLES AND RUNS	7
DRIBBLE COMPLETION	43%
DEFENDING	
TACKLES MADE	0
TACKLES WON	0%
BLOCKS	0
CLEARANCES	0
INTERCEPTIONS	1
DISCIPLINE	
FOULS	2
OFFSIDE	0

SECOND HALF

46 47 48 49 50 51 52 53 54 55 56 57 5 71 72 73 74 75 76 77 78 79 80 81 82 83 84 85 86 87 88 89 90

A foul on Michael Owen by Ashley Cole results in a free-kick. Danny Murphy finds Emile Heskey's head but he is denied only by a superb save from David Seaman in the Arsenal goal.

Henry fails to beat Sander Westerveld with his shot and Ashley Cole's side-footed follow-up is then cleared off the goal line by Liverpool captain Sami Hyypia.

Arsenal goal hero Ljungberg holds off Steven Gerrard

A low clearance is picked up by Robert Pires. He passes to Ljungberg, who rounds Sander Westerveld and puts the Gunners 1-0 up.

Jamie Carragher is fouled by Ray Parlour. Gary McAllister curls the free-kick into Arsenal's box and Markus Babbel heads it back from the far post. Michael Owen connects with a sensational scissor-kick volley on the six-yard line to fire it into the net. It's 1-1 and extra time looks likely.

Paddy plays a long ball over the top to find Michael and he runs towards the Arsenal goal. He holds off Lee Dixon and Tony Adams and with his left foot shoots past Seaman. Liverpool have done it!

MANAGEMENT

picture *mark leech*

> "I have not come here to finish third, I've come here to win the title – that is the eventual target"

GERARD **HOULLIER**
D.O.B 3.9.1947
BIRTHPLACE Therouanne, France
JOINED LIVERPOOL July 1998
PREVIOUS CLUBS Le Touquet, Noux-les-Mines, Lens, Paris St Germain, France

Gérard Houllier was an unknown 26-year-old teacher when he began coaching. He worked at Le Touquet and Arras before joining Noux-les-Mines, guiding the part-timers to promotion and success over Nantes in the French Cup.

He went to Lens in 1982, a team he took from the fourth to the first division, before leaving to join Paris St Germain in 1985, winning the title the next year. He then moved to the French national side, helping them to World Cup glory in 1998.

Gérard combines an ability to spot and sign high-quality players with a brilliant tactical knowledge. He also brought new ideas, training methods and strong discipline to Anfield when he took over in 1998.

Houllier has a great love of the club and was already a fan, having stood on the Kop while working as a teacher in the city in his early twenties. His first game at Anfield was Liverpool's 10-0 thrashing of Dundalk in the Fairs Cup in 1969.

"I have been a Liverpool fan since the 1970s," says Gérard. "It was a daunting task when I came here and I am constantly reminded of the past. But I have not come here to finish third, I've come to win the title – that is the eventual target."

BOSS, GAFFER, MANAGER. WHATEVER YOU WANT TO CALL HIM, MR HOULLIER HAS ALREADY GUIDED THE REDS TO A TREBLE TOGETHER WITH HIS RIGHT-HAND MEN...

PHIL **THOMPSON**

D.O.B 21.1.1954	
BIRTHPLACE Liverpool, England	
JOINED LIVERPOOL Feb 1971 (as player)	
PREVIOUS CLUBS Liverpool, Sheffield United (as player)	

SAMMY **LEE**

D.O.B 7.2.1959	
BIRTHPLACE Liverpool, England	
JOINED LIVERPOOL April 1976 (as player)	
PREVIOUS CLUBS Liverpool, QPR, Osasuna (Spain), Southampton, Bolton (as player)	

JOE **CORRIGAN**

D.O.B 18.11.1948	
BIRTHPLACE Manchester, England	
JOINED LIVERPOOL Summer 1994	
PREVIOUS CLUBS Manchester City, Brighton (as player)	

Assistant manager Phil Thompson is a Liverpool legend. Thommo was one of the club's greatest defenders and was captain when Liverpool won the European Cup in 1981.

Playing 466 games for the Reds, he also added another European Cup, seven League championships, an FA, Uefa and two League Cups to his impressive list of honours.

He was reserve coach at Liverpool in the early nineties but left during Graeme Souness' time as boss.

Invited back to Anfield when Gérard Houllier took sole charge, Phil is hoping to see a repeat of the success he enjoyed as a player.

He is credited with working with the manager to tighten up Liverpool's defence, transforming it into one of the meanest back fours in Europe.

"I show passion for the team and I don't like defeat. I want to see the shirt worn in the right manner, 100 per cent commitment and a will to win at all costs."

Sammy Lee is also a Red through and through. Another former great, he played in the Liverpool midfield between 1977 and 1986, picking up six League titles, two European Cups and four League Cups in 286 games for the Reds.

He worked as the reserve team coach at Anfield until Gérard Houllier promoted him to work with the first team.

"We all have a part to play here," says Sammy. "The backroom staff are all very close, we laugh and cry together. This is a dream job for me, I love being out on the training field every day. With this squad I know we can do things and the players and fans deserve more success."

Left-to-right: Sammy, Phil, Gérard and Joe with the Uefa Cup

Big Joe Corrigan is Liverpool's goalkeeping and reserves coach. As a keeper he was one of the best in the country, playing for Manchester City, Brighton and England.

Since joining the club in 1994 he has used his great experience to help the likes of Sander Westerveld, Pegguy Arphexad and Jorgen Nielsen to improve their game. Joe also became the reserve team coach in 1998 and in his first season saw Liverpool win the Premier reserve league for the first time in a decade.

"I'm honoured to be a part of the backroom staff," says Joe. "As soon as the offer came along for me to be Liverpool's first full-time goalkeeping coach I had no hesitation. Every day is enjoyable at this club. There are times when the rain is lashing down, but I still love it."

TEENAGE KICKS

pictures *anton want*

IT'S NOT JUST THE FIRST TEAM THAT'S LEADING THE WAY IN EUROPE. LIVERPOOL'S ACADEMY IN KIRKBY IS THE ENVY OF THE CONTINENT AND THE CLUB IS HOPING TO ONE DAY FIND ANOTHER OWEN OR GERRARD...

Ever wondered where Stevie G and Michael learned their skills? Well both are products of Liverpool's superb youth development system and graduates of the club's fantastic Soccer Academy in Kirkby.

The facility has everything that is needed to help produce a future crop of Anfield stars, including an ultra-modern indoor sports hall, 13 outdoor pitches, changing rooms, pools, video rooms and a gym.

It's not all football though, as the young players also have access to computers to provide them with skills for life outside of the game. There are also classes on health, fitness, diet and nutrition – such information is valuable to any player wanting to reach the top.

Players are usually aged between nine and 19 years and come to the Academy from all over the country. All receive top-quality coaching in the hope that one day they might make the grade and break through into the first team.

The Academy is run by the Reds' legendary former international winger Steve Heighway, who says, "The facilities at the Academy are really first class. The staff both here and at the club are really proud of what we do. The boys work hard and our aim is to get more of them ending up at Anfield one day."

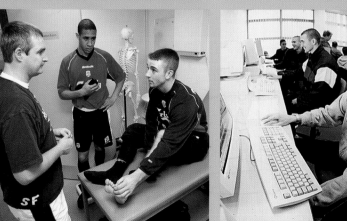

EUROPEAN UNION

THE REDS' STAR PLAYERS WEREN'T ALL BORN IN BRITAIN. SOME GREW UP IN COUNTRIES AS FAR AWAY AS CROATIA AND THE CZECH REPUBLIC...

FRANCE

FRENCH REDS
Bernard Diomède, Djimi Traore, Grégory Vignal

CAPITAL Paris

CHAMPIONS Nantes

FOOTIE FACT
Although French league football is not as strong as in Italy, England or Spain, the country's national side are World Cup holders and European Champions. Gérard Houllier helped make them the best team on earth when he worked for the French Football Federation.

HOLLAND

DUTCH RED
Sander Westerveld

CAPITAL The Hague

FOOTIE FACT
Like us, Ajax have won four European Cups.

FINLAND

FINNISH REDS
Jari Litmanen, Sami Hyypia

CAPITAL Helsinki

FOOTIE FACT
Jari is a national hero in Finland, where most people prefer ice hockey to football. He and Sami lined up for Finland against England at Anfield in March 2001.

GERMANY

GERMAN REDS Didi Hamann, Christian Ziege, Markus Babbel

CAPITAL Berlin

CHAMPIONS Bayern Munich

FOOTIE FACT
Germany is one of the strongest football nations in the world. They have won both the European Championship and World Cup on three occasions. German clubs are also doing well – Bayern Munich have just won the European Cup for the fourth time.

CZECH REPUBLIC

CZECH REDS
Patrik Berger, Vladimir Smicer

CAPITAL Prague

CHAMPIONS Sparta Prague

FOOTIE FACT
The Czech Republic surprised everyone to make it to the final of Euro 96 at Wembley. They lost to Germany in extra-time.

SWITZERLAND

SWISS RED
Stephane Henchoz

CAPITAL Berne

FOOTIE FACT
The Swiss ranked 3rd in the world in 1994.

CROATIA

CROATIAN RED
Igor Biscan

CAPITAL Zagreb

FOOTIE FACT
Croatia came third in the 1998 World Cup.

LIVERPOOL CROSSWORD

HOW MUCH DO YOU KNOW ABOUT LIVERPOOL FOOTBALL CLUB? LET'S PUT YOU TO THE TEST. GRAB A PEN, READ THROUGH THE CLUES ON THE RIGHT AND THEN WE'LL DISCOVER JUST HOW GOOD YOU REALLY ARE IN THE BOX…

SEE PAGE 60 FOR ANSWERS

ACROSS

1 It's where we play (7)
3 Brilliant young Scouse midfielder, _____ Gerrard (6)
4 He's big, he's Dutch, we like him very much, Sander _____ (10)
7 The scores are not odd, they're _____ (4)
8 When neither side wins it's a _____ (4)
10 It's Hamann with a nickname (4)
12 German defender, pure class at right back, Markus _____ (6)
15 Scored a screamer in last season's win over Manchester United at Old Trafford, _____ Murphy (5)
16 Skilful left-sided Czech midfielder, Patrik _____ (6)
17 Liverpool's record signing. A striker known for his DJ goal celebrations, Emile _____ (6)

DOWN

1 Liverpool reserve goalkeeper, Pegguy _____ (8)
2 We call him God or Robbie (6)
3 When the keeper stops the ball he makes a _____ (4)
5 Liverpool's French international winger, Bernard _____ (7)
6 He's the boss, Gérard _____ (8)
9 Brilliant central midfielder and club captain, Jamie _____ (8)
11 Hallelujah! He's scored another goal, Michael _____ (4)
12 If you're a defender, you play at the _____ (4)
13 Liverpool's most successful manager ever, ___ Paisley (3)
14 Finnish superstar striker, signed from Barcelona last season, _____ Litmanen (4)

Completed crossword answers (handwritten):
Across: 1 ANFIELD, 3 STEVEN, 4 WESTERVELD, 7 EVEN, 8 DRAW, 12 BABBEL, 15 DANNY, 16 BERGER, 17 HESKEY
Down: 1 ARPHEXAD, 2 FOWLER, 3 SAVE, 5 DIOMEDE, 6 HOULLIER, 9 CARRAGHER, 11 OWEN, 12 BACK, 13 BOB, 14 JARI

BOY WONDER

MICHAEL OWEN GETS HIS HANDS ON THE FA CUP AFTER SCORING TWO LATE GOALS TO WIN THE FINAL FOR IVERPOOL IN CARDIFF

 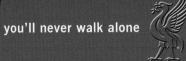
DEFENDERS

"We're now confident of winning every game we play. My one big dream is to win the Premiership with Liverpool. I am very passionate about this football club and I badly want us to succeed"

MARKUS **BABBEL**

D.O.B	8.9.1972
BIRTHPLACE	Munich, Germany
HEIGHT	1.80m
TRANSFER FEE	Free transfer
LIVERPOOL DEBUT	19 August 2000 vs Bradford City
PREVIOUS CLUBS	Hamburg, Bayern Munich
INTERNATIONAL SIDE	Germany

STEPHANE **HENCHOZ**

D.O.B	7.9.1974
BIRTHPLACE	Billens, Switzerland
HEIGHT	1.83m
TRANSFER FEE	£3.5million
LIVERPOOL DEBUT	21 September 1999 vs Hull City
PREVIOUS CLUBS	Xamax Neuchatel, Hamburg, Blackburn Rovers
INTERNATIONAL SIDE	Switzerland

In his first season with Liverpool, Markus wasted no time in settling into one of the meanest defences in Europe. The elegant defender won over the fans very quickly with his top-class defending and tireless attacking runs down the right wing.

Six goals on the way to the treble show that he is willing to help his team in any way he can. His opening goal in that amazing Uefa Cup final capped a superb display where he showed his versatility by switching to the centre of defence.

Markus has total belief in the team and says, "We are now confident of winning every game. My one big dream is to win the title with Liverpool. I am very passionate about this football club and I badly want us to succeed. It was always my dream to play in English football and as soon as I decided to leave Bayern Munich I was only ever going to move to one club."

Stephane forms one half of the most feared central defensive partnerships around. Alongside Sami Hyypia, the Swiss international has formed the bedrock of the team and they've even been compared to the legendary Reds defensive duo of Alan Hans tackling and blocking.

Stephane says, "No one could have predicted at the start of last season that we'd win three trophies. It's a clear sign of the progress we've made. We're a good team and I think we can get even better. We have a lot of talent here at Anfield, but the fact is that our squad is still very young."

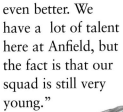

pictures steve orino

A MAJOR REASON BEHIND LIVERPOOL'S SUCCESS HAS ALWAYS BEEN A ROCK-SOLID DEFENCE. HERE'S WHY OUR BOYS AT THE BACK ARE AMONG THE VERY BEST...

SAMI **HYYPIA**

D.O.B	7.10.1973
BIRTHPLACE	Porvoo, Finland
HEIGHT	1.92m
TRANSFER FEE	£3 million
LIVERPOOL DEBUT	7 August 1999 vs Sheffield Wednesday
PREVIOUS CLUBS	MyPa-47, Willem II
INTERNATIONAL SIDE	Finland

JAMIE **CARRAGHER**

D.O.B	28.1.1978
BIRTHPLACE	Bootle, Liverpool
HEIGHT	1.80m
TRANSFER FEE	Signed as trainee
LIVERPOOL DEBUT	8 January 1997 vs Middlesbrough
INTERNATIONAL SIDE	England

> "Can we challenge for the title? I think we've had the players for a good few years now but it's about that winning mentality"

For some time it had been obvious that the Reds needed a commanding centre back. Fans wanted someone like the legendary Alan Hansen – comfortable on the ball and capable of organising the backline. When the unknown Sami Hyypia signed in 1999, some were not convinced that a solution had been found.

Sami's exceptional defensive skills soon came to the fore in 1999/00. In the air or on the ground, his ability to lead the team with an ice-cool temperament impressed many and he was Liverpool's player of the season in his first term. The Finn was just as brilliant last season.

Sami says, "I am obviously very pleased and proud with how it all ended last season. We had a lot of work to do, we stuck together, played well and got the right results. The fans are so pleased and we are very delighted for them – they deserve the success."

The 2000/01 season witnessed local hero Jamie Carragher's amazing breakthrough into the first team. The player was ever-present in a variety of positions, but he made the left back slot his very own.

Jamie showed great versatility and maturity and was made captain for the game against Sunderland at Anfield in September 2000.

The player exceeded all expectations, easily taking care of such feared wingers as David Beckham and Roma's Cafu.

Looking to the future, Jamie says, "Can we challenge United for the title? I think we've got the players. I think we have had the players here for a good few years now but it's about developing that winning mentality. Now that we've won those first few trophies, that might give us a bit more belief to go on from there."

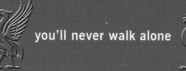

DEFENDERS

"When a team with the history and talent of Liverpool comes in for you, you don't turn them down"

GREGORY **VIGNAL**	
D.O.B 19.7.1981	
BIRTHPLACE Montpellier, France	
HEIGHT 1.78m	
TRANSFER FEE £500,000	
LIVERPOOL DEBUT 6 January 2001 vs Rotherham United	
PREVIOUS CLUBS Montpellier	
INTERNATIONAL SIDE France u-18	

CHRISTIAN **ZIEGE**	
D.O.B 1.2.1972	
BIRTHPLACE Berlin, Germany	
HEIGHT 1.86m	
TRANSFER FEE £5.5 million	
LIVERPOOL DEBUT 9 September 2000 vs Manchester City	
PREVIOUS CLUBS Bayern Munich, AC Milan, Middlesbrough	
INTERNATIONAL SIDE Germany	

Gérard Houllier looked to his native land to sign a player who has the potential to rise to the very top of the game.

Left back Grégory Vignal signed for Liverpool for £500,000 in September 2000 from Montpellier after being watched by a host of top teams.

After signing he said, "When a team with the history and talent of Liverpool comes in for you, then you don't turn them down."

Gregory has shown great attitude and performed well in the games he played for the Reds last season. One to watch.

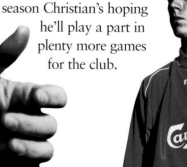

Blessed with supreme athleticism and a great left foot, Christian made a good start to his Liverpool career before a back injury kept him on the sidelines for two months.

Due to Carragher's impressive form at left back, Christian was pushed into the midfield to great effect in the Uefa Cup against Roma, but he has often found himself on the subs' bench.

"When you get a chance to sign for Liverpool you take it," said Christian. "It was a chance for me to play at the top level." Next season Christian's hoping he'll play a part in plenty more games for the club.

DJIMI **TRAORE**

D.O.B 1.3.1980	
BIRTHPLACE Laval, France	
HEIGHT 1.89m	
LIVERPOOL DEBUT 14 September 1999 vs Hull City	
PREVIOUS CLUBS Laval	
INTERNATIONAL SIDE France u-16	

VEGARD **HEGGEM**

D.O.B 13.7.1975	
BIRTHPLACE Trondheim, Norway	
HEIGHT 1.78m	
SENIOR DEBUT 16 August 1998 vs Southampton	
PREVIOUS CLUBS Rosenborg	
INTERNATIONAL SIDE Norway	

STEPHEN **WRIGHT**

D.O.B 8.2.1980	
BIRTHPLACE Liverpool	
HEIGHT 1.83m	
TRANSFER FEE Signed as trainee	
LIVERPOOL DEBUT 29 November 2000 vs Stoke City	
INTERNATIONAL SIDE England u-21	

When Gérard Houllier signed Djimi from French junior club Laval in February 1999, he stated, "In years to come the people of Liverpool will thank me for signing him."

The youngster arrived with the reputation of being the new Marcel Desailly – tall, quick and very confident on the ball.

The Worthington Cup presented Djimi with his senior debut against Hull City in 1999. But his hard work in the reserves saw him promoted to a regular starting position in the first team at left back for the first two months of 2000/01.

Djimi is fully committed to the Reds and says, "I love it at Liverpool. I've progressed and people have said I'm one for the future. That doesn't stop me wanting to win my place earlier than that. I want to play in as many matches as possible for Liverpool so that I can become a regular."

One of the few disappointments of 2000/01 was the continued absence of Vegard Heggem through injury. The attacking right back made only four appearances.

When fit, he is a lightning-quick and skilful attacking option who can fit in anywhere down the right.

Vegard says, "Everyone is pulling in the same direction, we have a good manager and we all want to win more trophies. When I signed, my biggest dream in life was to be successful at this club."

Stephen Wright has been earmarked as one of Liverpool's best ever home-grown defenders.

Like many Reds players, he can play in a variety of positions, although he admits that the centre of defence is his favourite.

The strong Liverpool back line has made it very difficult for the big defender to break in to the senior squad. Despite this, Stephen is a regular in the England u-21 set-up and he made his Liverpool debut in the 8-0 demolition of Stoke in the Worthington Cup in November after coming on as a sub.

Three months later Stephen made his Premiership debut against West Ham United, setting up a goal for his boyhood hero, Robbie Fowler in a 3-0 win at Anfield.

UEFA CUP FINAL

WHEN WEDNESDAY 16 MAY 2001
WHERE WESTFALENSTADION, DORTMUND, GERMANY
SCORE LIVERPOOL 5 ALAVES 4
(after extra-time)

THE REDS' FIRST EUROPEAN FINAL FOR 17 YEARS TURNS OUT TO BE A CLOSE-RUN THING, DECIDED AFTER 117 MINUTES BY A DRAMATIC GOLDEN GOAL THAT GAVE LIVERPOOL VICTORY AND A UNIQUE CUP TREBLE.

UEFA CUP FINAL TIMELINE FIRST HALF

SECOND HALF

1 2 3 **4** 5 6 7 8 9 10 11 12 13 14 15 **16** 17 18 19 20 21 22 23 24 25 26 **27** 28 29 30 31 32 33 34 35 36 37 38 39 40 **41** 42 43 44 45 46 47 **48** 49 50 **51** 52 53 54 55 56 57 58 59 60

A Gary McAllister free-kick finds an attacking Markus Babbel, who heads past Herrera in the Alaves goal and Liverpool go 1-0 up. A fantastic start for the Reds.

Michael Owen splits the Alaves defence with an intelligent pass to Steven Gerrard, who calmly rifles the ball home at the near post.

Contra gets forward, crosses it and Alonso is there with his head to pull one back for Alaves. Only fine saves from Westerveld deny Alaves two more.

Michael Owen loses his marker and Didi Hamann slides the ball to him. As he runs towards goal, the Alaves keeper makes an untidy challenge and deliberately trips the Liverpool striker in the box. Gary McAllister makes no mistake from the spot. Liverpool go in 3-1 up at half time and the game looks to be won.

Early on in the second half, Contra goes past Henchoz, crosses and Moreno makes it 3-2 with a header.

Gary McAllister fouls Moreno and the resulting free-kick is drilled hard and low underneath a jumping Liverpool wall, leaving Sander with no chance. The game is level at 3-3.

It's the stuff that dreams are made of: the Reds win the treble in Dortmund

Liverpool are given a dream start with a Markus Babbel-headed goal. Stevie G quickly adds another, but before the half-hour Alaves pull one back. Gary McAllister then converts a penalty and the Reds go in at half time with a 3-1 lead.

In the second half Alaves find the net twice to level the scores. But Robbie Fowler comes off the bench and takes the game to 4-3 with a truly fantastic right-footed strike.

With just two minutes to go, Jordi Cruyff heads in an Alaves equaliser. Extra-time must be played, with the game to be decided by a golden goal, or worse still, penalties.

After 117 minutes a dangerous Gary McAllister free-kick forces an own goal from Alaves' Geli and Liverpool have completed the treble!

Gary's moment of glory was well-earned after his fine performance

MAN OF THE MATCH GARY McALLISTER	
MINUTES ON PITCH	117
GOAL ATTEMPTS	
GOALS	1
SHOTS ON TARGET	1
SHOTS OFF TARGET	1
BLOCKED SHOTS	2
PASSING	
GOAL ASSISTS	2
TOTAL PASSES	53
PASS COMPLETION	85%
CROSSING	
TOTAL CROSSES	11
CROSS COMPLETION	9%
DRIBBLING	
DRIBBLES AND RUNS	5
DRIBBLE COMPLETION	40%
DEFENDING	
TACKLES MADE	4
TACKLES WON	75%
BLOCKS	0
CLEARANCES	0
INTERCEPTIONS	0
DISCIPLINE	
FOULS	0
OFFSIDE	0
YELLOW CARDS	1
RED CARDS	0

EXTRA-TIME

61 62 63 64 65 66 67 68 69 70 71 72 73 74 75 76 77 78 79 80 81 82 83 84 85 86 87 88 89 90 91 92 93 94 95 96 97 98 99 100 101 102 103 104 105 106 107 108 109 110 111 112 113 114 115 116 117 118 119 120

Robbie, on for Emile Heskey, receives the ball on the edge of the Alaves box, goes past defender Karmona and puts the Reds back in the lead with a sensational right-footed finish.

Sander Westerveld and Steven Gerrard fail to reach Contra's corner and Jordi Cruyff equalises with a dramatic last-minute header. The game must now go to extra-time.

Liverpool put pressure on Alaves keeper Herrera

Following a bad challenge on Vladimir Smicer, a second Alaves player is sent off and the Reds are awarded a free-kick. Gary McAllister's cross is deflected into the Alaves net by Delfi Geli and Liverpool win the Uefa Cup for the third time in the club's history.

ANFIELD LEGENDS

JOHN BARNES
'DIGGER' 1987 – 1997

Attributes Superbly skilful and quick winger, left-sided, great dribbler, free-kick specialist and scorer of many spectacular goals

Born Kingston, Jamaica 1963

Position Forward/midfielder

Games/Goals 407/108

International Caps/Goals 79/11 for England

Did you know? John won the PFA footballer of the year award in 1988 and the Football Writers' player of the year in 1988 and 1990

IAN CALLAGHAN
'CALLY' 1960 – 1978

Attributes Right-sided attacking midfielder, excellent crosser and passer of the ball, great tackler – a dependable and consistent player

Born Liverpool 1942

Position Midfielder

Games/Goals 857/69

International Caps/Goals 4/0 for England

Did you know? Ian joined as a schoolboy in 1957 and in three decades played in a record 640 League games for the Reds

RAY CLEMENCE
'CLEM' 1967 – 1981

Attributes A truly world-class goalkeeper. Brave, quick, athletic and very agile with exceptional concentration during games

Born Skegness 1948

Position Goalkeeper

Games/Goals 665/0

International Caps/Goals 61/0 for England

Did you know? In the 1978/79 season, aided by a water-tight defence, Ray conceded just 16 goals in 42 League games – still a record

KENNY DALGLISH
'KING KENNY' 1977 – 1991

Attributes A truly world-class goalscorer and provider, very skilful, clever and absolutely lethal with the ball at his feet in front of goal

Born Glasgow 1951

Position Forward/midfielder

Games/Goals 515/172

International Caps/Goals 102/30 for Scotland

Did you know? In his first season as player/manager Kenny led the Reds to an FA Cup and League championship double in 1985/86

ALAN HANSEN
'JOCKY' 1977 – 1991

Attributes Very classy, ball-playing defender, outstanding reader of the game, excellent tackler, great going forward, cool-headed

Born Sauchie, Clackmannanshire 1955

Position Defender

Games/Goals 620/14

International Caps/Goals 26/0 for Scotland

Did you know? Despite playing in one of the Reds' best-ever defences, Alan was initially rejected as a trialist at Anfield in August 1971

ROGER HUNT
'SIR ROGER' 1958 – 1969

Attributes Superstar striker from the 1960s, a record-breaking goalscorer, very strong, highly skilful, quick and tireless

Born Golbourne, Lancashire 1938

Position Centre forward

Games/Goals 492/286

International Caps/Goals 34/18 for England

Did you know? Roger was top scorer at Anfield for nine out of the ten seasons he was there. Also helped England win the World Cup in 1966

READING LIKE A HISTORICAL WHO'S WHO OF FOOTBALL, MANY OF THE GAME'S ALL-TIME GREATS HAVE WORN THE FAMOUS RED OF LIVERPOOL. HERE ARE JUST SOME OF THOSE LEGENDS FROM DAYS GONE BY...

KEVIN KEEGAN
'MIGHTY MOUSE' 1971 – 1977

Attributes Superstar striker from the 1970s, fearless, very fast and energetic, great finisher with his head or either foot

Born Doncaster 1951

Position Centre forward

Games/Goals 323/100

International Caps/Goals 63/21 for England

Did you know? Kevin was voted PFA player of the year in 1982 and European footballer of the year for two seasons running in 1978 and 1979

ALAN KENNEDY
'BARNEY RUBBLE' 1978 – 1985

Attributes Tough tackling left back, fast, liked to get forward, a great striker of the ball, known for his swashbuckling style

Born Sunderland 1954

Position Defender

Games/Goals 357/20

International Caps/Goals 2/0 for England

Did you know? Alan scored the winning goal in two European Cup finals for the Reds, against Real Madrid in 1981 and Roma in 1984

BILLY LIDDELL
'KING BILLY' 1938 – 1961

Attributes Excellent with either foot, athletic and strong, a very hard hitter of the ball, Billy was a hard-working model professional

Born Dunfermline 1922

Position Forward

Games/Goals 537/229

International Caps/Goals 28/6 for Scotland

Did you know? Billy served in the RAF during World War II. After football he went on to become a youth worker and lay preacher

STEVE McMANAMAN
'MACCA' 1990 – 1999

Attributes Free-running winger, enormously skilful on either flank, very quick, a brilliant dribbler of the ball, amazing fitness levels

Born Liverpool 1972

Position Midfielder

Games/Goals 364/66

International Caps/Goals 33/3 for England

Did you know? In the 1995 Coca-Cola Cup final Steve scored two superb goals against Bolton Wanderers to help Liverpool to victory

IAN RUSH
'RUSHIE' 1980 – 1996

Attributes Phenomenal goalscorer, also a hard-working centre forward with lightning pace, the club's record marksman

Born St Asaph, North Wales 1961

Position Centre forward

Games/Goals 660/346

International Caps/Goals 73/28 for Wales

Did you know? In 1983/84 Ian scored 47 goals in 64 appearances for the Reds and won the Golden Boot as Europe's leading goalscorer

GRAEME SOUNESS
'SOUEY' 1978 – 1984

Attributes Inspirational captain, commanding and very tough, also stylish and creative, an excellent passer and striker of the ball

Born Edinburgh 1953

Position Midfielder

Games/Goals 359/56

International Caps/Goals 54/4 for Scotland

Did you know? Graeme's last game for Liverpool was the 1984 European Cup final, when he lifted the trophy as skipper

SUPERQUIZ

JUST HOW MUCH OF A LIVERPOOL BRAINBOX ARE YOU? THE QUESTIONS BELOW WILL TEST YOUR KNOWLEDGE OF YOUR FAVOURITE TEAM WHILE THE PICTURE PAGE WILL CHALLENGE YOUR POWERS OF OBSERVATION...

1 Which striker scored five goals for Liverpool in the 2000/01 FA Cup competition and also scored the Reds' first goal last season?

2 The Reds played Barcelona and Alaves in last season's Uefa Cup competition, but which country do both of these teams come from?

3 Which big Dutch striker left Liverpool for Germany's SV Hamburg last season?

4 Against which club did Michael Owen score his first goal for Liverpool as a substitute way back in May 1997?

5 How many times have Liverpool won the FA Cup?

6 The Reds defeated only one Premiership club on their way to winning the Worthington Cup. Can you name this London team?

7 Who was the only Red to play in every Premiership game for Liverpool in season 1999/00?

8 In which year did Gérard Houllier become joint manager of Liverpool?

9 Who were the only team to beat Liverpool in both Premiership fixtures last season?

10 Who was the last Liverpool player to score in an international game at Anfield?

7) This Liverpool player appeared in every single Premiership game in 1999/00, but can you identify him?

11 Name the only Liverpool player to have scored 100 Premiership goals so far.

12 Who scored Liverpool's winning goal against Manchester United at Old Trafford last season?

13 Which country do Sami Hyypia and Jari Litmanen both play for?

14 Which club did Liverpool defeat by a record away score of 8-0 in last season's Worthington Cup?

15 Who scored Liverpool's last-minute winner in last season's derby match at Goodison?

16 From which club did Liverpool sign midfielder Dietmar Hamann?

17 Which current Liverpool player has won the most caps with England's under-21 side?

18 Can you name Liverpool's assistant manager?

19 What is the name of Liverpool's reserve goalkeeper?

20 Which England international midfielder signed for Liverpool from Everton in 2000?

21 Team-mates Patrik Berger and Vladimir Smicer play for which international team?

22 Which Swiss international player did Liverpool sign from Blackburn Rovers in 1999/00?

23 Who scored Liverpool's opening goal in last season's 2-0 victory over Manchester United at Anfield?

24 Liverpool's club captain failed to play in a single game in 2000/01 due to a severe injury, but can you name him?

25 Which German international defender signed for Liverpool from Bayern Munich last season?

SEE PAGE 60 FOR ANSWERS

FACE OFF

THIS FACE IS MADE UP OF FOUR PLAYERS, CAN YOU NAME THEM?

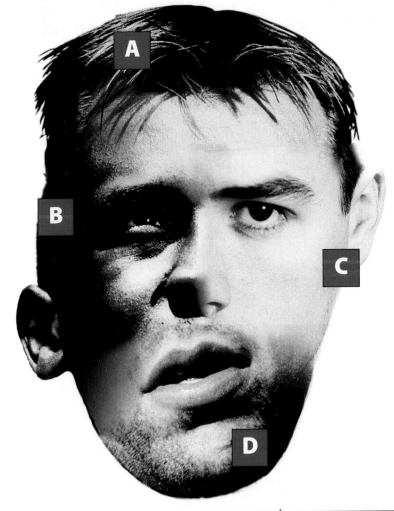

A: Sander Westerveld
B: Hes Key
C: Michael Owen
D: Babbel

IN THE PICTURE

CAN YOU GUESS WHICH PLAYERS ARE FEATURED BELOW?

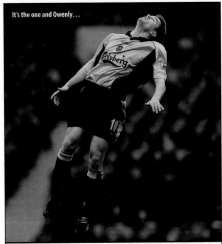

It's the one and Owenly...

ANSWER: Michael Owen

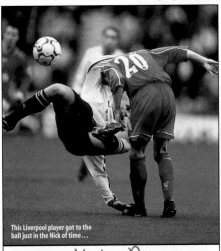

This Liverpool player got to the ball just in the Nick of time...

ANSWER: Nick Barmby

Which Liverpool player has just been Fowled?

ANSWER: Robbie Fowler

This Scouse midfielder takes off after another great strike

ANSWER: Steven Gerrard

Didi mean to end up on the Manchester United bench?

ANSWER: Didi Hammann

HOW TO...

THEY MAKE IT LOOK EASY. WHICH IS WHY THEY'RE WORLD-CLASS

SHOOT
LIKE STEVEN GERRARD

"At the start of last season, I would not have been too confident shooting from a long way out, but I had some joy with scoring and I always reckon I have got a good chance of finding the back of the net now. I've skied a few into the Kop in my time, but the trick is to keep your eye on the ball, keep over it and keep it down low when you strike."

SHIELD
LIKE EMILE HESKEY

"Strikers have to do a lot more than just score goals these days as it is a real team game now. It's all about leading the line and keeping possession for team-mates to come and support you in attack. One asset to my game is strength, I can hold the ball up under pressure from defenders by being able to keep my body between the ball and opponent."

PASS
LIKE GARY McALLISTER

"I've always regarded myself as a good passer of the ball, and it's important to have players in a team who can keep the ball moving and we've got a few at Liverpool. Sometimes you just have to make the simple pass to keep possession and there's nothing wrong with that, it's better than giving the ball away. But I'm still learning and looking to improve all the time myself."

LIKE JARI LITMANEN

"The important thing is to stay cool, make your decision about where you're going to put it and don't change your mind. I enjoy the responsibility of taking penalties though all the pressure is on the taker because no one expects the keeper to save it. My first Liverpool goal was from the spot against Sunderland. It was a great moment for me and if the chance comes to take more I'll do it."

TACKLE
LIKE STEPHANE HENCHOZ

"If you go sliding into tackles, you do yourself no favours and run the risk of conceding a free-kick or giving your opponent the chance to slide the ball past and get nearer to the goal. Instead, you need to stay on your feet as long as possible and try to shepherd him away. You must be strong and confident that you can outwit your opponent, especially with last-ditch tackles."

TAKE FREE-KICKS
LIKE DANNY MURPHY

"A couple of seasons ago I was having a bit of bad luck, the ball was flying wide or hitting the post but I was always confident I'd find the back of the net one day! When you take a free-kick, you have to work the goalkeeper – hitting the wall is a complete waste of a good position. If you get the shot on target and at least force a save then you've done your job."

GOAL**KEEPERS**

SANDER **WESTERVELD**
D.O.B 23.10.1974
BIRTHPLACE Enschede, Holland
HEIGHT 1.90m
TRANSFER FEE £4 million
SENIOR DEBUT 7 August 2000 vs Sheffield Wednesday
PREVIOUS CLUBS FC Twente, Vitesse Arnhem
INTERNATIONAL SIDE Holland

"It would mean the world to me if I was the keeper who helped Liverpool once again reach the top of English football"

Sander Westerveld has brought some much-needed stability to the defence and the big Dutchman has quickly established himself as one of the best keepers around.

For many Liverpool supporters Sander's most memorable performance was in the Worthington Cup final last season, when he saved two penalties in the tense shoot-out against Birmingham.

Sander has made giant strides playing for the Dutch national side. He appeared in Euro 2000 and is very close in the pecking order to first-choice keeper Edwin van der Sar. He remains focused on his Anfield career though, saying, "It's an honour to play here. It would mean the world to me if I was the keeper who helped Liverpool once again reach the top of English football."

WITH SO MANY FANTASTIC STRIKERS AROUND IT'S VITAL TO HAVE A GOALKEEPER WHO'S UP TO THE TEST. THE REDS ARE BLESSED WITH THREE OF THE VERY FINEST...

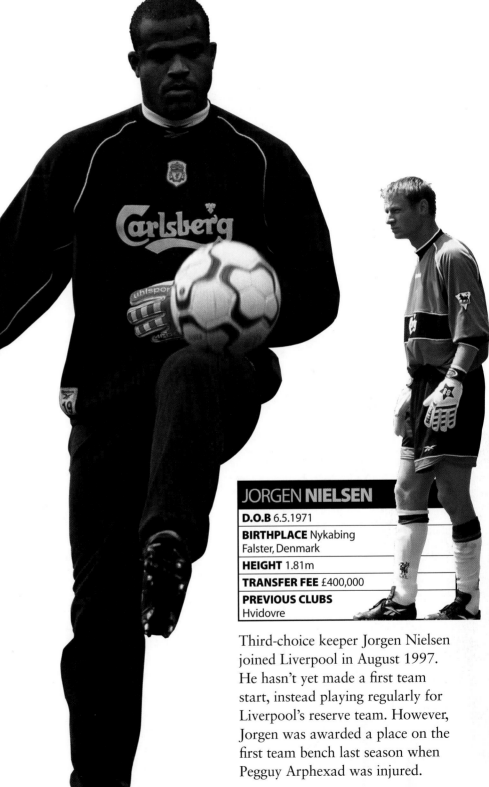

PEGGUY **ARPHEXAD**

D.O.B	18.5.1973
BIRTHPLACE	Abymes, Guadeloupe
HEIGHT	1.86m
TRANSFER FEE	Free
SENIOR DEBUT	1 November 2000 vs Chelsea
PREVIOUS CLUBS	Lens, Leicester City

Gérard Houllier moved quickly to sign Pegguy Arphexad from Leicester City in July 2000 after the Guadeloupean put on a fantastic display while playing against Liverpool at the end of the 1999/00 season.

Since his arrival at Anfield Pegguy has played just two first team games for the club, both in the Worthington Cup. But he refuses to feel down about his role as backup keeper, promising, "I'm working as hard as I can and I'm waiting patiently for my chance to come along. Liverpool are one of the most famous clubs in the world and even though I knew I wouldn't play every week I still knew I had to make the move."

"Liverpool are one of the most famous clubs in the world and even though I knew I wouldn't play every week I still knew I had to make the move"

JORGEN **NIELSEN**

D.O.B	6.5.1971
BIRTHPLACE	Nykabing Falster, Denmark
HEIGHT	1.81m
TRANSFER FEE	£400,000
PREVIOUS CLUBS	Hvidovre

Third-choice keeper Jorgen Nielsen joined Liverpool in August 1997. He hasn't yet made a first team start, instead playing regularly for Liverpool's reserve team. However, Jorgen was awarded a place on the first team bench last season when Pegguy Arphexad was injured.

SUPPORT YOUR TEAM

THE ANSWERS

CAN YOU CLAIM TO BE AN ANFIELD SUPERBRAIN? IT'S TIME TO CHECK HOW MANY YOU ANSWERED CORRECTLY...

P27 WORDSEARCH SOLUTION

A	I	P	Y	Y	H	Z	B	V	I	G	N	A	L	X
A	K	C	W	B	E	Q	L	M	E	S	M	D	Q	O
J	S	T	D	A	N	N	Y	B	X	L	S	I	Y	U
A	H	D	W	Q	C	K	E	D	J	A	R	I	B	V
M	Z	A	B	L	H	I	K	W	A	E	E	F	M	Q
I	G	R	B	M	O	K	S	T	M	L	D	K	R	P
E	V	E	X	S	Z	H	E	Z	I	S	N	J	A	C
M	Z	T	Q	J	T	N	H	Y	E	X	A	L	B	H
I	N	S	W	X	R	K	D	V	X	D	S	H	G	R
C	E	I	Z	B	A	B	B	E	L	Q	C	H	S	I
H	V	L	N	S	O	R	J	Z	K	C	V	A	Q	S
A	E	L	A	H	R	O	B	B	I	E	T	M	W	T
E	T	A	A	Q	E	Z	P	S	G	T	X	A	V	I
L	S	C	K	H	X	L	M	R	O	A	W	N	T	A
F	P	M	E	B	E	R	G	E	R	K	E	N	M	N

P36 CROSSWORD SOLUTION

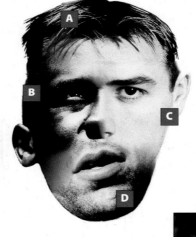

¹A	N	²F	I	E	L	D		³S	T	E	V	E	N	
R		O						A						
P		⁴W	E	S	T	E	R	V	E	L	⁵D		⁶H	
H		L						E			I		O	
⁷E	V	E	N								O		U	
X		R									M		L	
A											E		L	
⁸D	⁹R	A	W						¹⁰D	I	D	I		
	E								E				E	
	D		¹¹O										R	
	K		W											
	N		E		¹²B	A	B	¹³B	E	L			¹⁴J	
¹⁵D	A	N	N	Y		A		O					A	
	P					C		¹⁶B	E	R	G	E	R	
	P		¹⁷H	E	S	K	E	Y					I	

P48 SUPERQUIZ

1. Emile Heskey
2. Spain
3. Erik Meijer
4. Wimbledon
5. Six
6. Chelsea
7. Sami Hyypia
8. 1998
9. Leeds United
10. Michael Owen
11. Robbie Fowler
12. Danny Murphy
13. Finland
14. Stoke City
15. Gary McAllister
16. Newcastle United
17. Jamie Carragher
18. Phil Thompson
19. Pegguy Arphexad
20. Nick Barmby
21. Czech Republic
22. Stephane Henchoz
23. Steven Gerrard
24. Jamie Redknapp
25. Markus Babbel

P49 FACE-OFF

A. Sander Westerveld
B. Emile Heskey
C. Michael Owen
D. Markus Babbel

P49 IN THE PICTURE

1. Michael Owen
2. Nick Barmby
3. Didi Hamann
4. Steven Gerrard
5. Robbie Fowler

– JOIN TODAY

To join, call The Official Liverpool Supporters Club for an information pack on 0151 264 2290 (please ask an adult to phone for you), or write to The Official Liverpool Supporters Club, PO Box 205, Liverpool L69 4PS or visit www.liverpoolfc.tv and click on Fansforum and Supporters Clubs to print off and complete an application form.

You follow Robbie, Steven and Sami on match days, but if you become a junior member of The Official Liverpool Supporters Club you'll really get close to the heart of Liverpool FC.

That's because you'll enjoy discounts on official LFC gear and tours, and even get the chance to attend the exclusive 'Fans Day' event when the famous Anfield gates are opened just for members of The Official Liverpool Supporters Club.

You'll certainly get closer to the team then – watching a first team training session and seeing some of Liverpool's famous Old Boys. It's the stuff your dreams are made of.

Quite simply, The Official Liverpool Supporters Club is world class and if you want to be a world class junior supporter then you need to be a member.

Support your team - join today!

THE OFFICIAL LIVERPOOL SUPPORTERS CLUB

JUNIOR SUPPORTERS
ENJOY ALL THE FOLLOWING BENEFITS:

- Exclusive Liverpool FC geometry set and bookmark
- Exclusive workbook from Letts – football makes learning fun*
- Exclusive results wallchart
- Exclusive chance to become a team mascot
- Exclusive Cup Winner's cap
- An invite to attend the Liverpool FC Fans Day at Anfield
- A personalised membership card
- Free admission to reserve team matches
- Discount tours of the Museum & Stadium
- A unique collectible action postcard
- A specially designed Liverpool tin to keep your Club items in

*This item will be mailed separately during the course of your membership

Annual Fee £14